MEANS THIS MUCH TO ME

Coupon 1

LOVE COUPONS

KEEPING THE FIRE ALIVE

REDEEMABLE FOR ONE

BREAKFAST IN BED

CONDITIONS

Don't get up. Stay under the covers.
Waffles, scrambled eggs, or whatever your heart desires.

SIGN FOR REDEMPTION DATE

YOU MEAN THIS MUCH TO ME

Coupon 2

LOVE COUPONS

KEEPING THE FIRE ALIVE

REDEEMABLE FOR ONE

YES DAY

CONDITIONS

In a world of challenges, you deserve one full YES DAY to
rejuvinate. So ask away and expect YES as an answer.

SIGN FOR REDEMPTION DATE

YOU MEAN THIS MUCH TO ME

Coupon 3

LOVE COUPONS

KEEPING THE FIRE ALIVE

REDEEMABLE FOR ONE

DINNER AND A MOVIE

CONDITIONS

Let's make it a night. Pick the restaurant and pick the movie.

SIGN FOR REDEMPTION DATE

YOU MEAN THIS MUCH TO ME

LOVE COUPONS

LOVE COUPONS

LOVE COUPONS

LOVE COUPONS
KEEPING THE FIRE ALIVE

REDEEMABLE FOR ONE

A WEEKEND GETAWAY

CONDITIONS

Where should we go? You decide and we can make it a weekend we'll both remember.

SIGN FOR REDEMPTION DATE

YOU MEAN THIS MUCH TO ME

LOVE COUPONS
KEEPING THE FIRE ALIVE

REDEEMABLE FOR ONE

NIGHT ON THE TOWN

CONDITIONS

The world's your oyster. Put on your best dress and let's hit the town for a unforgettable adventured.

SIGN FOR REDEMPTION DATE

YOU MEAN THIS MUCH TO ME

LOVE COUPONS
KEEPING THE FIRE ALIVE

REDEEMABLE FOR ONE

DAYTIME DATE

CONDITIONS

Wanna skip the lines and the crowd. Let's go out when everyone else is at work. Just you and me.

SIGN FOR REDEMPTION DATE

YOU MEAN THIS MUCH TO ME

LOVE COUPONS

LOVE COUPONS

LOVE COUPONS

LOVE ❤ COUPONS
KEEPING THE FIRE ALIVE

REDEEMABLE FOR ONE

JUST ME AND YOU TIME

CONDITIONS

Sometimes we just need some "us" time. Now's that time.

SIGN FOR REDEMPTION — DATE

YOU MEAN THIS MUCH TO ME

LOVE ❤ COUPONS
KEEPING THE FIRE ALIVE

REDEEMABLE FOR ONE

FRIDAY NIGHT ~~DRINKS~~

CONDITIONS

How about you and me grabbing a little cocktail and enjoying some time out and about? Let's go.

SIGN FOR REDEMPTION — DATE

YOU MEAN THIS MUCH TO ME

LOVE ❤ COUPONS
KEEPING THE FIRE ALIVE

REDEEMABLE FOR ONE

LOVER'S QUARREL VICTORY

CONDITIONS

We may not always agree, but this coupon let's you win outright. Done. You're right.

SIGN FOR REDEMPTION — DATE

YOU MEAN THIS MUCH TO ME

LOVE COUPONS

LOVE COUPONS

LOVE COUPONS

KEEPING THE FIRE ALIVE

LOVE ❤ COUPONS

REDEEMABLE FOR ONE

A NICE QUIET NIGHT IN

CONDITIONS

For when staying home sounds better than going outside and dealing with the world. Home is where the heart is.

SIGN FOR REDEMPTION DATE

YOU MEAN THIS MUCH TO ME

KEEPING THE FIRE ALIVE

LOVE ❤ COUPONS

REDEEMABLE FOR ONE

A SENSUAL MASSAGE

CONDITIONS

You are my everything and deserve a great massage to relieve the stress of the day.

SIGN FOR REDEMPTION DATE

YOU MEAN THIS MUCH TO ME

KEEPING THE FIRE ALIVE

LOVE ❤ COUPONS

REDEEMABLE FOR ONE

AN EROTIC MASSAGE

CONDITIONS

Let's not forget that the next step above a SENSUAL MASSAGE is an EROTIC MASSAGE. Pass the oil and put a smile on your face.

SIGN FOR REDEMPTION DATE

YOU MEAN THIS MUCH TO ME

LOVE 🔥 COUPONS

LOVE 🔥 COUPONS

LOVE 🔥 COUPONS

KEEPING THE FIRE ALIVE

LOVE COUPONS

REDEEMABLE FOR ONE

COOK AND CLEAN

CONDITIONS

Go change into something comfortable while I make you a great
meal and then clean up while you have a little "you" time.

SIGN FOR REDEMPTION DATE

YOU MEAN THIS MUCH TO ME

KEEPING THE FIRE ALIVE

LOVE COUPONS

REDEEMABLE FOR ONE

A NICE,
V FOOT RUB

CONDITIONS

Put up your feet and I'll do the rest. Trust me,
your little toes will thank you.

SIGN FOR REDEMPTION DATE

YOU MEAN THIS MUCH TO ME

KEEPING THE FIRE ALIVE

LOVE COUPONS

REDEEMABLE FOR ONE

ANY HOUSEHOLD
CHORE DONE

CONDITIONS

What's the one chore you hate to do around the house?
I've got this. Now go grab a good book and relax.

SIGN FOR REDEMPTION DATE

YOU MEAN THIS MUCH TO ME

LOVE COUPONS

LOVE COUPONS

LOVE COUPONS

LOVE COUPONS

KEEPING THE FIRE ALIVE

REDEEMABLE FOR ONE

ONE FUN SHOPPING SPREE

CONDITIONS

Choose the store or stores and I will be your wingman.
I promise to smile and cheer you on.

SIGN FOR REDEMPTION _____   DATE _____

YOU MEAN THIS MUCH TO ME

LOVE COUPONS

KEEPING THE FIRE ALIVE

REDEEMABLE FOR ONE

QUALITY CUDDLE TIME

CONDITIONS

Just us and some quality cuddling that will make
your friends jealous.

SIGN FOR REDEMPTION _____   DATE _____

YOU MEAN THIS MUCH TO ME

LOVE COUPONS

KEEPING THE FIRE ALIVE

REDEEMABLE FOR ONE

GO OUT DANCING

CONDITIONS

Let me knock the dust off my dancing shoes (or boots)
and we can go kick up our heels.

SIGN FOR REDEMPTION _____   DATE 1/1/25

YOU MEAN THIS MUCH TO ME

LOVE COUPONS

LOVE COUPONS

LOVE COUPONS

LOVE COUPONS

KEEPING THE FIRE ALIVE

YOU MEAN THIS MUCH TO ME

REDEEMABLE FOR ONE

A FANCY DINNER AT A FANCY RESTAURANT

CONDITIONS

Dinner is one thing. A fancy dinner is a whole other level.
Let's kick it up a notch.

SIGN FOR REDEMPTION DATE

LOVE COUPONS

KEEPING THE FIRE ALIVE

YOU MEAN THIS MUCH TO ME

REDEEMABLE FOR ONE

MOVIE NIGHT OF YOUR CHOICE

CONDITIONS

Have a movie that's on your watch-list? Let's go.
Popcorn and soda included.

SIGN FOR REDEMPTION DATE

LOVE COUPONS

KEEPING THE FIRE ALIVE

YOU MEAN THIS MUCH TO ME

REDEEMABLE FOR ONE

SPEND AN EVENING STARGAZING

CONDITIONS

The best, long-running show of all time happens every night
above our heads. Meet me for a night of stargazing.

SIGN FOR REDEMPTION DATE

LOVE 🔥 COUPONS

LOVE 🔥 COUPONS

LOVE 🔥 COUPONS

LOVE COUPONS

KEEPING THE FIRE ALIVE

REDEEMABLE FOR ONE

WRITE A ROMANTIC LETTER OR POEM

CONDITIONS

How do I love thee? Let me count the ways and write a letter or a poem.

SIGN FOR REDEMPTION

DATE

YOU MEAN THIS MUCH TO ME

LOVE COUPONS

KEEPING THE FIRE ALIVE

REDEEMABLE FOR ONE

A WHOLE EVENING OF JUST CUDDLING

CONDITIONS

Dinner's over and we have the whole evening to snuggle and cuddle to our heart's delight.

SIGN FOR REDEMPTION

DATE

YOU MEAN THIS MUCH TO ME

LOVE COUPONS

KEEPING THE FIRE ALIVE

REDEEMABLE FOR ONE

PRETEND IT'S OUR FIRST DATE

CONDITIONS

Do you remember that spark and excitement of our first date? Let's rekindle that magic.

SIGN FOR REDEMPTION

DATE

YOU MEAN THIS MUCH TO ME

LOVE 🔥 COUPONS

LOVE 🔥 COUPONS

LOVE 🔥 COUPONS

LOVE COUPONS

KEEPING THE FIRE ALIVE

REDEEMABLE FOR ONE

ONE STRIPTEASE

CONDITIONS

Turn on some swanky music. Dim the lights.
And let me remind you of how much of a hunk I am.

SIGN FOR REDEMPTION DATE

YOU MEAN THIS MUCH TO ME

LOVE COUPONS

KEEPING THE FIRE ALIVE

REDEEMABLE FOR ONE

ONE KNOCK-ME-OFF-MY-FEET KISS

CONDITIONS

Pucker up and brace yourself.

SIGN FOR REDEMPTION DATE

YOU MEAN THIS MUCH TO ME

LOVE COUPONS

KEEPING THE FIRE ALIVE

REDEEMABLE FOR ONE

WRITE 10 THINGS YOU LOVE ABOUT ME

CONDITIONS

Only ten things? Simple.
The challenge is ranking them.

SIGN FOR REDEMPTION DATE

YOU MEAN THIS MUCH TO ME

LOVE COUPONS

LOVE COUPONS

LOVE COUPONS

LOVE COUPONS

KEEPING THE FIRE ALIVE

REDEEMABLE FOR ONE

PLAYING SEXY DRESS UP

CONDITIONS

May be used with the FANCY DINNER AT A FANCY RESTAURANT coupon.
Either way, let me be your arm-candy in or out of the house.

SIGN FOR REDEMPTION DATE

YOU MEAN THIS MUCH TO ME

LOVE COUPONS

KEEPING THE FIRE ALIVE

REDEEMABLE FOR ONE

ROMANTIC BUBBLE BATH FOR TWO

CONDITIONS

Any room in there for two?
Let the bubbles flow...or overflow.

SIGN FOR REDEMPTION DATE

YOU MEAN THIS MUCH TO ME

LOVE COUPONS

KEEPING THE FIRE ALIVE

REDEEMABLE FOR ONE

FUN WITH CHOCOLATE BODY PAINT

CONDITIONS

Can I paint you a picture with you as my delicious canvass?
Let's let our creative sides out.

SIGN FOR REDEMPTION DATE

YOU MEAN THIS MUCH TO ME

LOVE 🔥 COUPONS

LOVE 🔥 COUPONS

LOVE 🔥 COUPONS

LOVE COUPONS

KEEPING THE FIRE ALIVE

REDEEMABLE FOR ONE

KISS AND CUDDLE BY THE FIRE

CONDITIONS

By the smile on your face I take it you approve of this little trifecta of happiness: kiss, cuddle, and fire.

SIGN FOR REDEMPTION DATE

YOU MEAN THIS MUCH TO ME

LOVE COUPONS

KEEPING THE FIRE ALIVE

REDEEMABLE FOR ONE

ONE WILD FANTASY FULFILLED

CONDITIONS

You know that one thing, nudge-nudge, the one thing that makes you blush and your heart race. Yes, that.

SIGN FOR REDEMPTION DATE

YOU MEAN THIS MUCH TO ME

LOVE COUPONS

KEEPING THE FIRE ALIVE

REDEEMABLE FOR ONE

ANYWHERE. ANYTIME.

CONDITIONS

Really. No questions asked. All you have to do is invite me and I will stop in my tracks and drop everything.

SIGN FOR REDEMPTION DATE

YOU MEAN THIS MUCH TO ME

LOVE COUPONS

LOVE COUPONS

LOVE COUPONS

BONUS: And just in case we didn't cover everything, here's 11 extra coupons. Let's just call them "**Wild Cards.**" As in, go ahead and get wild and creative with these cards!

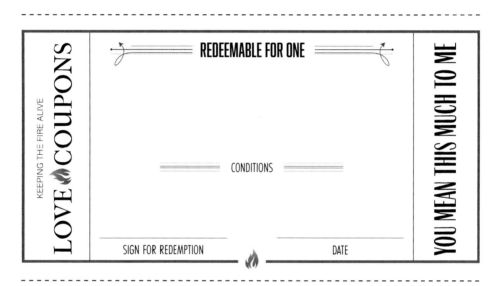

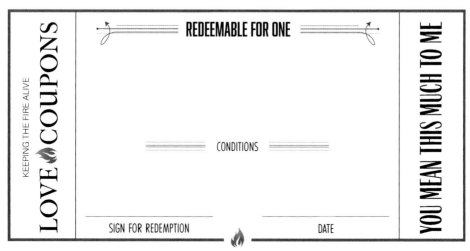

LOVE COUPONS

LOVE COUPONS

LOVE COUPONS

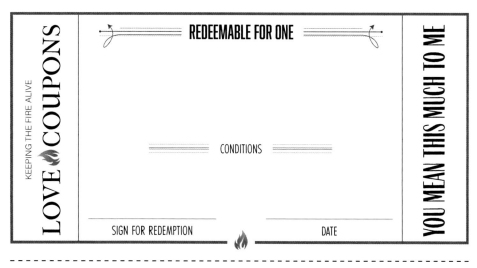

LOVE COUPONS

KEEPING THE FIRE ALIVE

REDEEMABLE FOR ONE

CONDITIONS

SIGN FOR REDEMPTION

DATE

YOU MEAN THIS MUCH TO ME

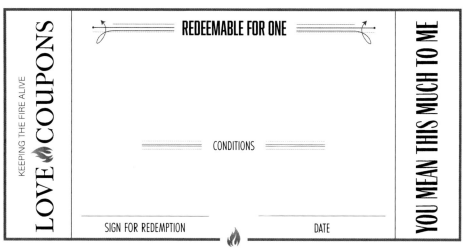

LOVE COUPONS

KEEPING THE FIRE ALIVE

REDEEMABLE FOR ONE

CONDITIONS

SIGN FOR REDEMPTION

DATE

YOU MEAN THIS MUCH TO ME

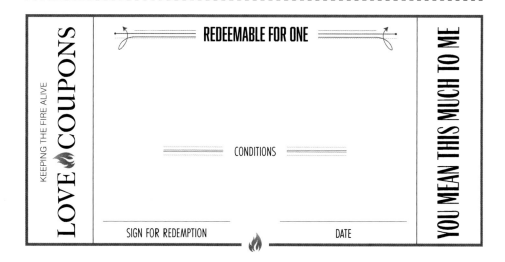

LOVE COUPONS

KEEPING THE FIRE ALIVE

REDEEMABLE FOR ONE

CONDITIONS

SIGN FOR REDEMPTION

DATE

YOU MEAN THIS MUCH TO ME

LOVE COUPONS

LOVE COUPONS

LOVE COUPONS

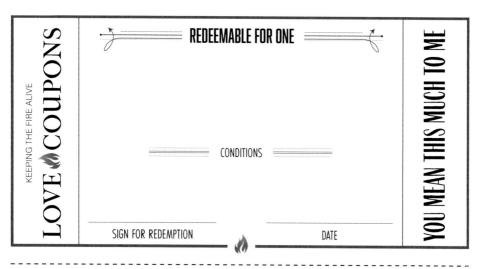

LOVE COUPONS

KEEPING THE FIRE ALIVE

REDEEMABLE FOR ONE

CONDITIONS

SIGN FOR REDEMPTION

DATE

YOU MEAN THIS MUCH TO ME

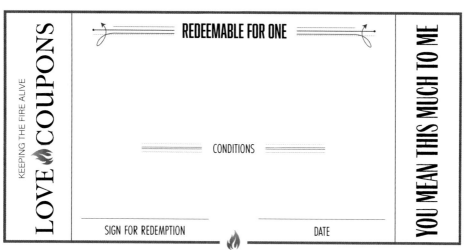

LOVE COUPONS

KEEPING THE FIRE ALIVE

REDEEMABLE FOR ONE

CONDITIONS

SIGN FOR REDEMPTION

DATE

YOU MEAN THIS MUCH TO ME

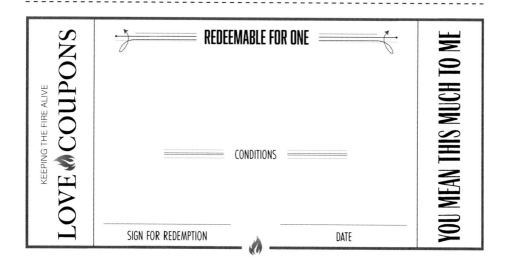

LOVE COUPONS

KEEPING THE FIRE ALIVE

REDEEMABLE FOR ONE

CONDITIONS

SIGN FOR REDEMPTION

DATE

YOU MEAN THIS MUCH TO ME

LOVE COUPONS

LOVE COUPONS

LOVE COUPONS

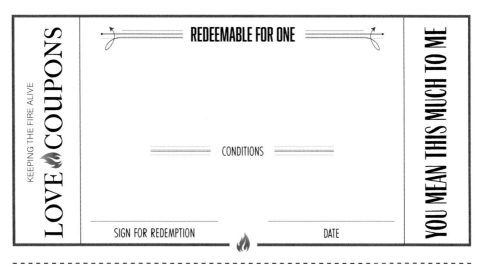

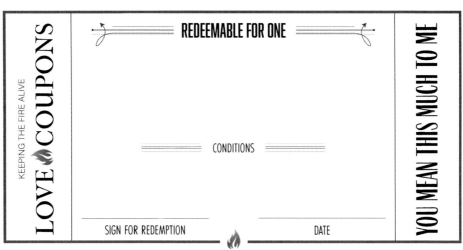

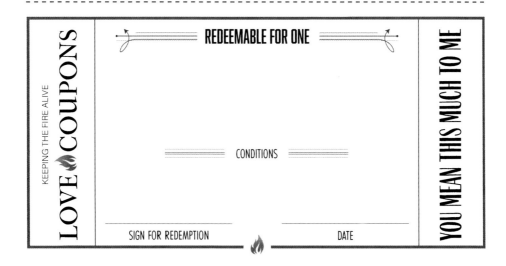

LOVE🔥COUPONS

LOVE🔥COUPONS

LOVE🔥COUPONS